EDGE
BOOKS

DIRT BIKES

James Stewart

Motocross Great

by Terri Sievert

Consultant:

Alex Edge
Associate Editor
MotorcycleDaily.com

Capstone
press

Mankato, Minnesota

Edge Books are published by Capstone Press,
151 Good Counsel Drive, P.O. Box 669, Mankato, Minnesota 56002.
www.capstonepress.com

Library of Congress Cataloging-in-Publication Data
Sievert, Terri.
    James Stewart : motocross great / by Terri Sievert.
    p. cm.—(Edge books. dirt bikes)
    Summary: "Traces the life and career of motocross racing star James 'Bubba'
Stewart"—Provided by publisher.
    Includes bibliographical references and index.
    ISBN 0-7368-4365-5 (hardcover)
    1. Stewart, James, 1985– —Juvenile literature. 2. Motorcyclists—United States—
Biography—Juvenile literature. 3. Motocross—Juvenile literature. I. Title. II. Series.
GV1060.2.S84S54 2006
796.7'5'092—dc22   2005005813

Editorial Credits
Connie Colwell Miller, editor; Jason Knudson, set designer; Kate Opseth,
    book designer; Wanda Winch, photo researcher; Scott Thoms, photo editor

Photo Credits
Frank Hoppen, cover, 7, 17
Getty Images Inc./Jeff Kardas, 18, 20
Steven Bruhn, 5, 6, 8, 11, 13, 14, 15, 21, 23, 25, 27, 28

1 2 3 4 5 6 10 09 08 07 06 05

Table of Contents

CHAPTER 1

A Young Star

In June 2004, 18-year-old James "Bubba" Stewart sped his motorcycle down a hill at High Point Raceway in Mount Morris, Pennsylvania. A rut at the bottom of the hill had caused many other riders problems. The rut knocked them off balance and forced them to slow down.

James didn't slow down. He swung his right leg over the bike and leaned to the right. He balanced on the toe of his left boot and steered the bike uphill. James didn't realize he was doing a special move to speed through the rut. He just reacted to the track.

Learn about:
- Exciting style
- Practicing to be great
- African American star

James is skilled at handling tracks that cause other riders problems.

James is not afraid of crashing.

Creative Style

James has a fast and flashy riding style. He likes to fly high over jumps. He speeds around the curves. Some people think he is reckless. He sometimes crashes in races because he tries new moves. But his winning streak proves that the style works for him.

James hopes his style will bring more fans to supercross. He wants people in the stands to love the races. James likes to point to the crowd after winning a race. He encourages fans to cheer loudly by putting his hand to his ear. He gives out high fives as he rides past fans on the sidelines.

James often points to the crowd or makes hand signals during moves.

James likes to entertain the fans at races.

A Young Legend

James is a talented motorcyclist. Difficult moves seem easy for him. He enjoys taking risks and is not afraid to crash. While still in his teens, he had success that other riders can only dream about.

Practice is important in all sports, and James knows this. He spent hours training to become great. He rode until he had learned how to handle any situation on his bike.

James is the first African American motocross star. He has been compared to baseball's Jackie Robinson and golf legend Tiger Woods. But James doesn't feel that being African American sets him apart from other riders. He just wants to win.

CHAPTER 2

Amateur to Pro

James was born in Bartow, Florida, on December 21, 1985. James' father raced motorcycles. He wanted his son to enjoy the sport as much as he did. James' father took him on his first motorcycle ride when he was only two days old.

James wanted to be just like his dad. By age 3, James was riding and racing ATVs. When he was 4 years old, he received a Yamaha 50 motorcycle for Christmas.

Learn about:
- An early start
- Top amateur
- On to pro

James loves riding motorcycles now as much as he did when he was young.

Learning to Race

James entered his first motorcycle race soon after receiving the motorcycle. He wasn't very good at first. But he loved to ride and he wanted to win.

People started noticing that James worked hard. He practiced until he improved. When James was 7, people at Kawasaki noticed his skills. This company became his sponsor.

James' parents supported him. They bought land near Haines City, Florida. They built tracks on the land so James could practice.

James also learned by watching other racers. Jeff "Chicken" Matiasevich was James' favorite rider. Some people say that James got his nickname when he started calling himself "Baby Chicken." Fans shortened "Baby Chicken" to "Bubba."

"I just go out there and race because I think we all look the same under a helmet."
—James Stewart

Kawasaki has been James' sponsor throughout his career.

James plans his race strategy before each race.

Turning Pro

By 2001, James had won more amateur championships than any other racer. In his final season as an amateur, he won every race he entered.

In January 2002, James was ready to turn pro. He started in the 125cc Supercross Series. He fell twice in his first pro race in Anaheim, California. But he still finished in second place.

His next pro race was in San Diego. James started the race in fourth place. He almost crashed. But he quickly caught up and passed the leader. James crossed the finish line and made history. He became the youngest person to win a supercross main event. He was only 16 years old. He was so excited that he almost started to cry.

It didn't take long for James to start winning.

CHAPTER 3

Winning Streak

In 2002, James continued his rookie season as one of the fastest riders in his class. He whipped around corners. He flew over jumps and smaller bumps called whoops. He had more wins than any other rider in the 125cc Supercross Series West Region. He finished second in the points standings. But James wanted to be first. Later that year, he turned to the 125cc Motocross Series.

Learn about:

- A new record
- Supercross champ
- More success

James is driven to win every race.

James was only 16 years old when he became an AMA national champ.

Training for Success

James knew he had what it took to be a champion. He continued to practice. He studied other riders and watched how they rode. He learned their moves and their racing styles.

All the practice paid off. In 2002, James won the opening motocross race in San Bernardino, California. He was the first rookie to win the AMA motocross event.

James' success continued. He won 10 of the 12 races in the AMA 125cc Motocross Series. At the time, this was the most wins any rider had ever had in a single season. At age 16, he became the AMA 125cc national motocross champion and was the first African American AMA champion. He was named the 2002 Rookie of the Year.

Continued Success

James continued to win. In 2003, he won seven supercross races and took the AMA 125cc Supercross Series West Region championship.

In 2003, James won the AMA 125cc Supercross Series West Region championship.

James did not let his shoulder injury keep him from racing.

In the final race of the series, James injured his shoulder. The injury kept him out of the first AMA Motocross Series races of the 2003 season. When he recovered, he won the final seven races. He finished third in the season standings.

CHAPTER 4

King James

In 2004, James continued to win. His 14th 125cc Supercross Series victory gave him the most first-place finishes of any rider in the 125cc class. He went on to win every supercross race he entered in 2004. He also took the 125cc Supercross Series East Region title. He became only the second rider to win a supercross title on both coasts.

Later that year, James dominated the AMA 125cc Motocross Series. He won 11 of the 12 events and won his second motocross championship.

Learn about:
- An exciting rider
- Flashy winner
- Moving up

In 2004, James won every supercross race he entered.

Career Statistics

Year	Class	Wins	Points	Finish
2002	AMA West Supercross 125cc	3	145	2nd
2002	AMA Motocross 125cc	10	529	1st
2003	AMA West Supercross 125cc	7	197	1st
2003	AMA Motocross 125cc	7	350	3rd
2004	AMA East Supercross 125cc	6	150	1st
2004	AMA Motocross 125cc	11	575	1st

Best in the Country

Next, James took on the best riders in the country at the East/West Shootout in Las Vegas, Nevada. This race was tougher than his other supercross races had been that year.

James was used to easy wins. This time, Stephane Roncada challenged him. Roncada took the lead after the first turn and led for three laps. James battled Roncada and finally passed him. James crossed the finish line first. He had proven himself to be the best rider in the nation in his class.

James had to take the lead away from Stephane Roncada (#21) to win the East/West Shootout.

Bubba Today

After his success in the 125cc class, James was ready to face tougher competition. In 2005, he moved up to the 250cc class in both supercross and motocross. In April, he became the first African American to win a 250cc supercross event.

James is also interested in other types of racing. He wants to race in Europe. He also might try supermoto, truck, or car racing.

James has proven that he is a top-notch racer. But his dreams for success already go beyond the track. He plans to have his own TV show.

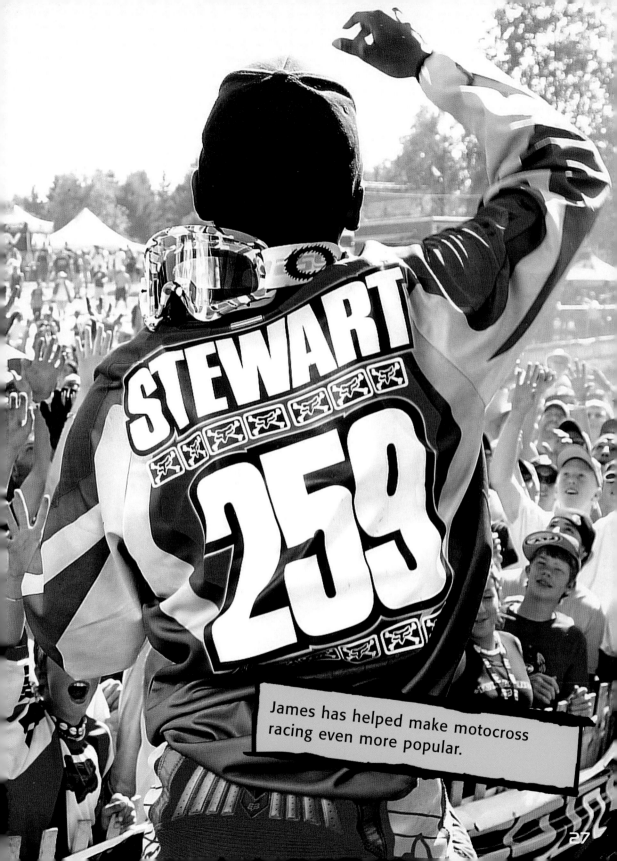

James has helped make motocross racing even more popular.

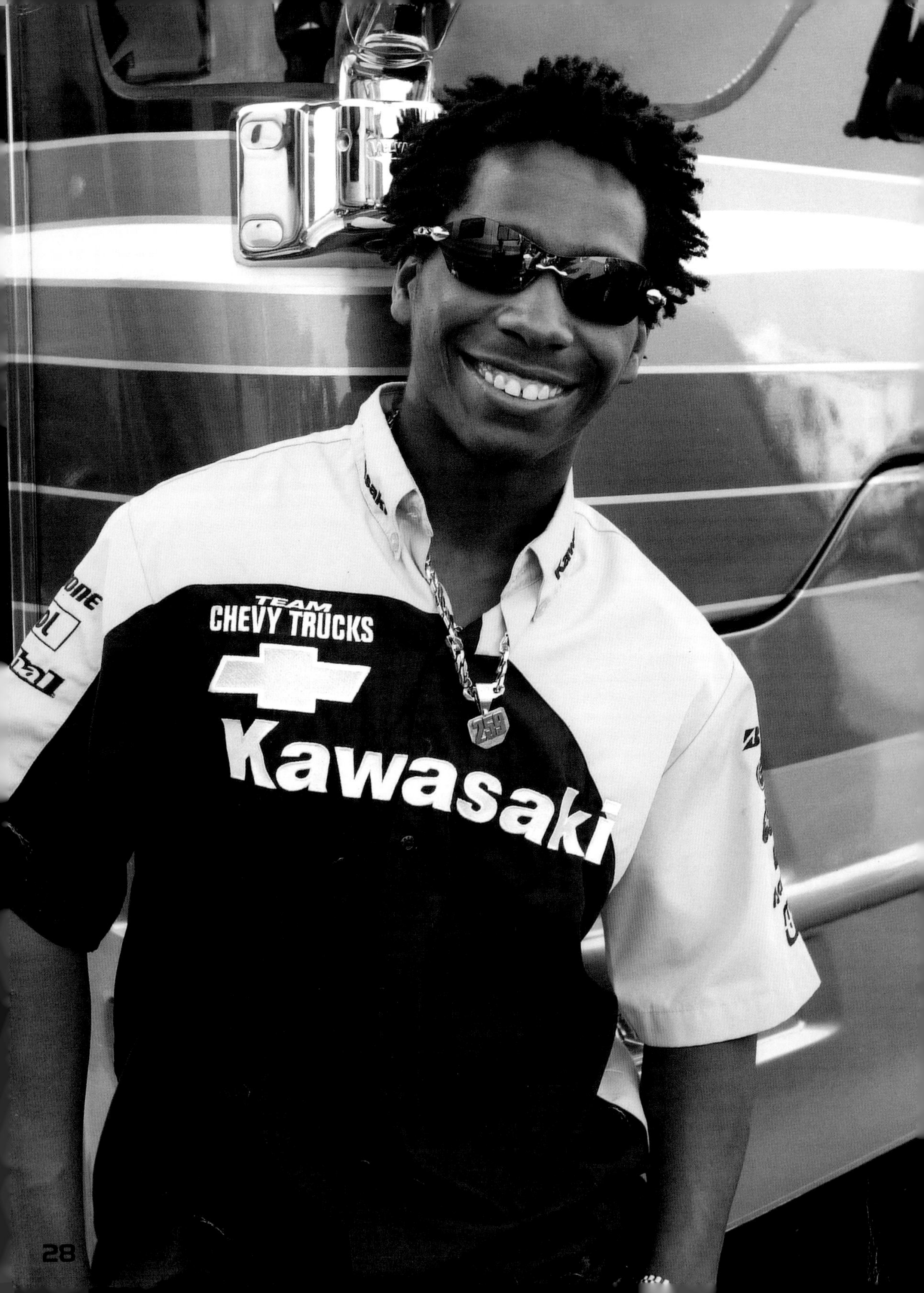
TEAM
CHEVY TRUCKS
Kawasaki
259

Career Highlights

1990 — James enters his first race at age 4.

1993 — James gets a sponsorship agreement with Kawasaki.

2001 — James ends his amateur career with a record-setting 11 AMA amateur national titles. He also sets a record for the most wins as an AMA amateur rider.

2002 — James wins a record-setting 10 AMA 125cc motocross events and takes the series championship title. He is named AMA Motocross/Supercross Rookie of the Year.

2003 — James wins the AMA 125cc West Region Supercross Championship.

2004 — James wins the AMA 125cc East Region Supercross Championship and the AMA 125cc Motocross Series Championship.

2005 — James becomes the first African American to win a 250cc supercross main event.

Glossary

amateur (AM-uh-chur)—an athlete who does not earn a living from competing in a sport

motocross (MOH-toh-kross)—a sport in which people race motorcycles on dirt tracks

sponsor (SPON-sur)—a company that gives money to an athlete in exchange for using and advertising the company's products

supercross (SOO-puhr-kross)—motorcycle races held on dirt tracks in a stadium

supermoto (SOO-puhr-moh-toh)—a sport in which dirt bikes race on tracks with both paved and dirt areas

Read More

Freeman, Gary. *Motocross.* Radical Sports. Chicago: Heinemann Library, 2003.

Herran, Joe, and Ron Thomas. *Motocross.* Action Sports. Philadelphia: Chelsea House, 2004.

Schaefer, A. R. *Motocross Cycles.* Wild Rides! Mankato, Minn.: Capstone Press, 2002.

Internet Sites

FactHound offers a safe, fun way to find Internet sites related to this book. All of the sites on FactHound have been researched by our staff.

Here's how:

1. Visit *www.facthound.com*
2. Type in this special code **0736843655** for age-appropriate sites. Or enter a search word related to this book for a more general search.
3. Click on the **Fetch It** button.

FactHound will fetch the best sites for you!

Index